ECHOES FROM THE ZEN GARDEN

20 Short Zen stories for Mindfulness, Self-reflection, Positive Thinking, and Achieving Inner Peace

By
EMILY HARPER

Copyright © 2025 EFKET LTD.

All Rights Reserved.

Table of Contents

Introduction 1

Section 1: Mindfulness 3
    Story 1: The Present Moment 5
    Story 2: The Mindful Monk 11
    Story 3: The Tea Ceremony 17
    Story 4: The Farmer's Patience 23
    Story 5: Breath of the Buddha 29

Section 2: Self-Reflection 35
    Story 1: The Mirror of the Mind 37
    Story 2: The Monk's Burden 43
    Story 3: The Two Arrows 49
    Story 4: The Empty Boat 55
    Story 5: The Gift of Insults 61

Section 3: Positive Thinking 67
    Story 1: The Sunlit Path 69
    Story 2: The Laughing Buddha 75
    Story 3: The Fortunate Misfortune 81
    Story 4: The Changing Seasons 87
    Story 5: The Full Bowl 93

Section 4: Inner Peace 99
    Story 1: The Silent Retreat 101
    Story 2: The Unmoved Mind 107
    Story 3: The Mountain's Stillness 113

Story 4: The Flowing River 119
Story 5: The Lotus in the Mud 125
Conclusion 131

Introduction

Welcome to Zen Whispers: Stories of Mindfulness and Serenity. In this book, you'll step into the lives of ordinary people from all walks of life—farmers, monks, artisans, and travelers—each navigating challenges, choices, and lessons that reveal the power of mindfulness, self-reflection, positive thinking, and inner peace. These stories are inspired by Zen philosophy, but their wisdom is universal, offering practical insights for anyone seeking balance, clarity, and joy in their everyday life.

Every day, we are faced with situations that test our patience, challenge our thinking, or weigh on our hearts. Some moments are small, like deciding how to respond to a kind gesture or choosing to pause during a busy day to enjoy the present. Others might be harder, like handling setbacks at work or finding calm amidst personal struggles. The stories in this book show that, no matter who you are or where you are in life, mindfulness and positivity can turn even the simplest acts into meaningful transformations.

Let's take a moment to think about what it means to live fully in the present. It's not about perfection or avoiding problems. Instead, it's about noticing the little things—the sound of the rain, the warmth of a kind word, or the steady rhythm of your breath. These moments of awareness, though small, have the power to bring us peace, gratitude, and a sense of purpose. And the best part? Mindfulness is a skill you can cultivate every day, no matter your circumstances.

As you read each story, imagine yourself in the place of the characters. What if you were Marco, learning to see opportunity in adversity? Or Haruto, finding gratitude in the simplicity of an empty bowl? Each character is on their own journey of growth, and their stories are filled with lessons that can help us all embrace life's challenges with wisdom and grace.

You'll find that every story is followed by a reflection section that makes it easy to connect the story's lessons to your own life. These reflections include:

• **Thought-Provoking Insights**: A short explanation of the story's core message to deepen your understanding.

• **A Question for Introspection**: A single, powerful question to help you reflect on your own thoughts, feelings, and actions.

• **Guidance for Application**: Practical tips to help you bring the story's lessons into your daily routine.

Each chapter is its own journey, introducing you to unique characters and new settings. From the serene gardens of Kyoto to the bustling streets of Seoul, these stories are woven with themes of resilience, gratitude, and the beauty of the present moment. Some characters face loss, others struggle with self-doubt, and still others learn to let go of anger or fear. Each one has something valuable to teach—about how to navigate life's challenges with compassion, awareness, and an open heart.

These stories remind us that even the smallest actions, like pausing to take a deep breath or choosing kindness in a difficult moment, can ripple outward, transforming not just our own lives but also the lives of those around us. When we live mindfully, we discover the strength to weather life's storms and the serenity to appreciate its blessings.

So, are you ready to begin? With every chapter, you'll meet characters who inspire, challenge, and encourage you to see life through the lens of mindfulness. Get ready to pause, reflect, and grow. Let's embark on this journey together—one story, one lesson, one moment at a time.

Section 1: Mindfulness

Story 1:
The Present Moment

In the verdant foothills of Japan's distant mountains, nestled within a small, almost forgotten village, there lived an elderly Zen master revered far and wide for his extraordinary tranquility and deep, profound wisdom. His name, whispered like a secret among those who sought enlightenment, was Master Saito. The tales of his understanding had traveled far beyond the village, reaching the ears of Kenji, a young and prosperous merchant plagued by relentless worries and fears that darkened his every success with shadows of doubt and sorrow.

Kenji's life, filled with the riches of commerce and the company of many, offered him no peace. His mind, a battleground of past regrets and future anxieties, could find no moment of stillness. He had tried all remedies suggested by his acquaintances—from philosophical readings to lavish vacations—yet nothing quelled his inner turmoil. Upon hearing of Master Saito's teachings, Kenji was driven by a newfound hope, a beacon of peace in the tempest of his existence. Determined, he embarked on a journey to the master's village, seeking what he could not give himself: a moment's peace in the torrent of time.

Arriving early one misty morning, when the dew still clung to the cobwebbed emerald leaves and the world seemed hushed and sacred, Kenji found Master Saito in the heart of a quaint garden, tending to his bonsai trees with the tender care of a parent to a child. The garden was a testament to patience and dedication, qualities that Kenji realized he sorely lacked.

With a respectful bow, Kenji approached and expressed his plight. "Master Saito, my life is full yet my heart is empty, troubled by thoughts that steal my present joys. How may I find the peace that eludes me?"

Master Saito, looking up from his delicate task, met Kenji's gaze with eyes as calm as the deepest ocean and as wise as the ancient hills that surrounded them. "Follow me," he invited, and led Kenji to a babbling brook that lay on the edge of his garden, where the gentle murmur of flowing water composed a natural melody.

They sat together on an old, worn bench, the wood cool and mossy beneath them. Master Saito gestured towards the brook. "Watch the water, Kenji. It flows by without concern for the past or fear of the future. It simply is. It encounters rocks and curves in its path, yet it presses onward, embracing each moment with grace and ease."

Kenji observed silently, noting how the water kissed every stone, every leaf that fell upon its surface, without ever clinging to anything.

"Your mind should be like this stream," Master Saito continued. "Free from the clutches of what has been and what is yet to come. Embrace now, for it is the only moment you truly have."

"How can I live as the water does?" Kenji asked, his voice tinged with the weight of unshed burdens.

"Begin with your breath," the master replied. "Breathe in deeply, and as you do, let your mind gather all your woes. Breathe out slowly, and with it, release them into the stream. Do this until you feel lighter, until you are merely a spectator of your thoughts, not a prisoner."

Kenji closed his eyes and breathed as instructed, each exhale a whisper of release, each inhale a gathering of resolve. They sat together through the morning, the only sounds the rustling of leaves and the steady, reassuring flow of the stream.

"Now, open your eyes and live as you breathe," said Master Saito, as the sun began its climb into the sky, casting a golden glow that set the brook alight with sparkling dances of light. "Let each action be deliberate and mindful, as you were with your breath. Whether you walk, eat, or speak, be fully present, as if each act is your last. This is the essence of mindfulness."

Kenji spent the day immersed in this new way of being. He walked through the garden, each step a meditation; he ate, each bite a symphony of flavors; he listened to the master, each word a lesson. As the day waned into the soft purple twilight of evening, a profound sense of peace settled over him, a peace that came from within, untouched by the external chaos of his earlier life.

Before he left, Kenji bowed deeply to Master Saito, gratitude filling his heart. "Thank you, master, for showing me the way. I came seeking peace for a moment, yet you have given me a way to find it at any moment."

Master Saito smiled, his eyes twinkling like stars in the dusk. "Remember, Kenji, peace is not a place to arrive at, but a manner of traveling. Mindfulness is your map; your heart, the compass. Use them well, and you will never be lost."

With a heart lighter than he had ever known, Kenji returned to his life, carrying with him the lessons of the brook and the bonsai, forever changed by the wisdom of a day spent in the presence of a master of mindfulness.

Thought-Provoking Insights

Living in the present is the cornerstone of mindfulness and inner peace. Like the flowing brook, which neither clings to the past nor fears the future, we, too, can find tranquility by embracing the now. Mindfulness allows us to step out of the chaos of our thoughts and into the simple, profound beauty of the moment.

Guidance for Application

1. Practice mindful breathing daily, focusing on each inhale and exhale to anchor yourself in the present.

2. Engage in your everyday activities—walking, eating, or even cleaning—with deliberate attention, noticing every detail.

3. When your mind wanders to worries or regrets, gently bring your focus back to the present, using your breath as a guide.

Question for Introspection

How often do you find yourself fully immersed in the present moment, free from distractions of the past or future?

Story 2:
The Mindful Monk

In the verdant valleys of rural Japan, where the mountains seem to hold the sky itself aloft, there lived a monk named Hoshin. Unlike many who sought seclusion for their spiritual journey, Hoshin chose to remain connected with the world, believing true mindfulness could be achieved amidst the bustle of life and not apart from it.

Hoshin was a beloved figure in his village, known for his profound presence and an uncanny ability to make everyone he met feel as though they were the sole focus of his attention. This rare quality drew people from far and wide, each seeking the peace that seemed to radiate from him like warmth from the sun.

One spring day, as cherry blossoms painted the village in shades of fleeting beauty, a young artist named Emiko approached the monk. She carried with her a canvas, her tools, and a heart heavy with the turmoil of unfulfilled potential. Her life, much like her canvas, felt blank, overshadowed by a cacophony of choices and unrealized dreams.

"Master Hoshin," Emiko began, her voice a mixture of reverence and desperation, "I am lost in the maze of my own life. How do you find peace in the moment when every moment seems filled with noise?"

Hoshin welcomed her with a gentle smile, suggesting they walk through the village as they talked. As they strolled, Hoshin's steps were measured and deliberate, each footfall a testament to his mindful approach to life.

"See the cherry blossoms," Hoshin said, pausing beneath a particularly lush tree. "They bloom brilliantly, fully present in their brief moment of glory without concern for the wind that will soon sweep their petals away. They do not cling to their beauty, nor do they dread their falling. They simply are."

Emiko listened, her gaze following a petal spiraling slowly to the ground. "But how can I learn to live like the cherry blossom? My mind is always rushing, always reaching for something just beyond."

"That is where mindfulness begins," Hoshin explained. "It starts with the simplest of acts—the way we breathe, the way we walk, the way we eat. Each act, done mindfully, brings us back to the present."

To illustrate his point, Hoshin led Emiko to a small teahouse at the village's edge. They sat in silence, preparing tea with meticulous attention to each detail. Each movement was an act of meditation, from the warming of the pot to the pouring of the green, steaming liquid into tiny cups.

"Mindfulness is this," Hoshin said as he handed a cup to Emiko. "It is being with this cup of tea, tasting each sip as if it were both the first and the last. It is allowing ourselves to be fully present with how the tea tastes, how it makes us feel, how it changes from moment to moment."

Emiko took a sip, and for the first time noticed the subtleties of the flavor, the warmth that spread through her, the fragrance that filled the air. It was as if the tea encapsulated a world she had never taken the time to explore.

"Now, apply this to your art," Hoshin continued. "Approach your canvas with the same presence you give to this tea. Let each stroke of your brush be like each sip—complete in itself."

The days turned into weeks, and Emiko began to practice mindfulness in every brush stroke, finding that as she did, her canvas began to fill not just with color, but with life. Her art transformed, as did her spirit, becoming expressions of the present moment.

Months later, as the cherry blossoms once again prepared to adorn the village, Emiko returned to Hoshin. This time, her canvas was vibrant, a riot of colors and emotions that mirrored the journey of her discovery.

"Master Hoshin," she said, her eyes bright with tears of gratitude, "you have taught me to find the silence beneath the noise, the peace within the chaos."

Hoshin looked at the painting, then at Emiko, and smiled. "You have learned well. Remember, the beauty of mindfulness is not in escaping life but in living it fully, one present moment at a time."

From that day on, Emiko's art became known not just for its beauty, but for its ability to capture the fleeting, precious essence of the present, just as the mindful monk had captured the hearts of those who sought his wisdom.

Thought-Provoking Insights

Mindfulness is the art of fully immersing oneself in the present, even amid life's noise and chaos. It allows us to slow down and savor each moment, just as the cherry blossom blooms with quiet beauty before its petals fall. By focusing on simple acts—like sipping tea or walking—we can discover profound peace and clarity. True mindfulness transforms ordinary moments into extraordinary opportunities to live with intention and awareness.

Guidance for Application

1. Choose one routine activity—such as drinking your morning coffee or brushing your teeth—and practice doing it mindfully, paying attention to every sensation.

2. When working on a task, focus solely on it, allowing yourself to engage fully without distraction.

3. Begin a mindfulness practice by dedicating a few minutes daily to simply observing your breath or surroundings, letting each moment unfold without judgment.

Question for Introspection

How can you bring mindfulness into a simple daily activity, such as eating or walking?

Story 3:
The Tea Ceremony

In the tranquil city of Kyoto, where ancient traditions breathe life into the daily rhythm, stood the renowned Ryokan Teien, a tea house cherished for its adherence to the centuries-old practice of the tea ceremony. Within its walls, draped in the scent of fresh tatami and the quiet murmur of the garden beyond, resided Aiko, the tea master, known throughout Japan for her profound ability to transform the ceremonial into a profound exercise of mindfulness.

On a brisk autumn day marked by the fluttering of golden leaves, a businessman from Tokyo, Taro, stepped through the aged bamboo gate of Ryokan Teien. Taro was a man accustomed to the electric pulse of a city that never sleeps; his days were a blur of numbers, negotiations, and networkings that stretched his nerves thin and left little room for stillness.

The tea house was a stark contrast to his world. Here, time seemed to slow, and even the air felt thicker, filled with a calm that Taro could almost reach out and touch. He was greeted by Aiko, whose smile held the peace of the ages, her presence a soothing balm to his frayed edges.

"Welcome, Taro-san," Aiko said, guiding him to the tearoom, a space that seemed untouched by time. "Today, you shall not just witness, but truly participate in the art of *chanoyu*, the Way of Tea, a journey into mindfulness."

Taro, feeling oddly out of place in his business attire amidst the simplicity of the tea room, watched as Aiko began the ceremony. The cleaning of the tools—a bamboo whisk, a scoop, a tea bowl—was done with meticulous care, each motion deliberate, fluid, and full of intent.

"Each movement in *chanoyu* is a meditation," Aiko explained softly, her hands pausing in their graceful dance. "Mindfulness is the heart of this ceremony. We are here, fully present, with every whisk, every pour, every sip. It is our escape from the endless rush of life."

As she spoke, Aiko prepared the matcha with an elegance that seemed to weave silence into the space between them. The vibrant green tea was whisked into a frothy elixir, the aroma alone enough to draw one deeper into the moment.

"Observe the tea, Taro-san," she invited, passing him the thick, warm bowl, her hands an extension of her heart. "Notice its color, its warmth. Sip it not just with your lips but with your whole being. Let it anchor you here, in the now."

Taro brought the bowl to his lips, the bitter taste of the matcha striking a contrast to its visual gentleness. It was complex, layered, demanding his full attention. Each sip was a discovery, an unfolding of nuances, mirroring the layers he built around his own life, his own truths.

"The way of tea teaches us that beauty and understanding lie in simplicity," Aiko continued, her voice a grounding force. "In these moments of stillness, we find the clarity that the noise of the world so often obscures."

The ceremony progressed slowly, each step a building block towards mindfulness. Aiko spoke of *ichigo ichie*, a cherished Japanese concept meaning "one time, one meeting," which encapsulates the idea that each encounter is unique and fleeting, thus should be deeply cherished.

"This moment," Aiko gestured to the space around them, "will never occur again. Nor will any moment in our lives. Like each meeting in this tearoom, each is an opportunity to be fully present."

As the ceremony drew to a close, Taro felt a shift within himself. The peace of the tearoom, the taste of the tea, the wisdom of Aiko's words, all wove together into a tapestry of mindfulness that he could take back with him to Tokyo.

Returning to his world, Taro carried the essence of *chanoyu* with him. The hustle of Tokyo's streets didn't slow, but his reaction to them did. He found moments of mindfulness in his daily activities—savoring his morning coffee with no phone in hand, listening more attentively in meetings, walking through the crowded streets and noticing the sky above him.

Taro's life transformed in subtle but profound ways. He approached each task, each interaction, as if it were both the first and the last of its kind, embracing *ichigo ichie*. His days became a series of moments, each lived fully, each a step on the path of mindfulness that Aiko had shown him.

Through the simple, deliberate acts of a tea ceremony, Taro discovered not just the art of tea, but the art of living. In the quiet space between each sip, between each breath, he found the stillness he had been seeking, a stillness that had always been there, waiting for him in the present moment.

Thought-Provoking Insights
The tea ceremony teaches us that mindfulness lies in the deliberate, intentional acts of daily life. Through simplicity and presence, we can find clarity and peace in even the smallest moments. Embracing the fleeting nature of life, as encapsulated in the concept of *ichigo ichie* ("one time, one meeting"), helps us cherish each encounter as unique and irreplaceable.

Guidance for Application

1. Choose one daily task, such as preparing a meal or having tea, and perform it with full attention, savoring each step as a mindful ritual.

2. Practice the principle of *ichigo ichie* by cherishing every interaction or experience as unique and unrepeatable.

3. Create small pauses in your day to reflect on the beauty of simplicity and be present in the moment, whether in nature, a conversation, or a quiet corner.

Question for Introspection

How can you transform a simple daily activity into an opportunity for mindfulness and presence?

Story 4:
The Farmer's Patience

In the fertile plains of rural Hokkaido, where the seasons paint the vast landscapes with vibrant hues, there lived a farmer named Isamu. Unlike the typical image of a weary farmer burdened by the toil of the land, Isamu carried an air of serene calmness and an almost contagious optimism. His farm, a modest plot of land inherited from generations before him, was his temple, his place of meditation, and his life's teacher.

One chilly morning at the cusp of spring, when the frost still whispered secrets to the dawn, a young university student named Keiko arrived at Isamu's farm. Keiko was researching sustainable farming practices for her thesis and had heard of Isamu's unique approach to agriculture, which emphasized mindfulness and patience above all else.

"Welcome, Keiko-san," Isamu greeted her with a warm smile, his eyes twinkling with the wisdom of the land. "You come seeking knowledge of the soil, but perhaps you will leave with knowledge of the soul as well."

Curious and eager, Keiko followed Isamu around the farm, noting his meticulous yet unhurried methods of planting and tending to his crops. There was a rhythm to his routine, a palpable respect for the natural order of things that Keiko had not seen in other, more mechanized farms.

As they walked between the neat rows of burgeoning green, Isamu began to share his philosophy. "Farming, like life, thrives on patience. We plant seeds and provide them with what we can—water, nutrients, care—but ultimately, we must wait. We must trust the earth, the rain, the sun. Mindfulness in farming means being present with this process, understanding its rhythms, and learning from its pace."

Keiko listened intently, scribbling notes as Isamu spoke. They stopped by a field where young sprouts were just beginning to nudge their way through the rich, dark soil. "See these sprouts? They are young, fragile, yet full of potential. I watch them, I nurture them, but

I do not rush them. I am mindful of their needs, their time to grow, which cannot be hurried."

The days turned into weeks, and Keiko's visits became regular. She observed Isamu's interactions with his crops, his animals, and even the wild birds that frequented his fields. It wasn't just his actions but his very presence that seemed to create a harmony with nature.

One afternoon, as a storm brewed on the horizon, Isamu took Keiko to a part of the farm she hadn't seen before. It was a small orchard of fruit trees that he had planted years ago. The trees were laden with blossoms, promising a bountiful harvest.

"As farmers, we face many challenges—storms, pests, diseases. Yet, each of these challenges is an opportunity to practice mindfulness," Isamu explained as they watched the dark clouds roll closer. "We observe, we respond, but we do not panic. We accept the things we cannot change, and we adapt to those we can."

The storm hit hard that evening, the winds howling like ancient spirits of the air. Keiko watched as Isamu calmly secured his tools and sheltered his animals. There was a steady sureness in his steps—a testament to his life's practice of mindfulness.

The next morning, the storm had passed, leaving behind a mess of fallen branches and scattered leaves. Yet, amidst the chaos, the blossoms on the trees remained largely intact. Isamu's preparations had mitigated much of the damage.

"This is what I mean, Keiko-san," Isamu said as they assessed the orchard. "Patience and mindfulness prepare us for the inevitable storms. They teach us resilience, allowing us to bloom even after hardship."

Months passed, and the season of harvest arrived. Keiko helped Isamu with the harvest, experiencing the joy of reaping what had been sown with such patience and care. Each fruit, each vegetable held a story, a lesson in mindfulness that Isamu imparted to her.

On her last day at the farm, as Keiko prepared to return to university, she felt a profound sense of gratitude and a newfound understanding of mindfulness. Isamu gifted her a basket of fruits from the orchard, each piece a symbol of the lessons she had learned.

"Remember, Keiko-san, mindfulness is not just a practice for the quiet moments of meditation; it is a way of living," Isamu advised, his voice gentle yet firm. "Carry this mindfulness back to your world. Let it grow in you as these seeds grow in the soil—patiently, resiliently, beautifully."

Keiko left the farm with more than just data for her thesis. She carried with her the seeds of mindfulness that Isamu had sown in her spirit, seeds that would continue to grow throughout her life, enriching her every moment with the patience and presence she had witnessed in the heart of Hokkaido's farmlands.

Thought-Provoking Insights

The farmer's approach to patience and mindfulness teaches us that life, like farming, requires trust in the natural rhythms of growth and change. Challenges, much like storms, are inevitable, but they also bring opportunities to adapt and strengthen. By being present, nurturing what we can, and accepting what we cannot control, we cultivate resilience and find peace in the process of growth.

Guidance for Application

1. Approach tasks with patience and presence, focusing on the process rather than rushing toward outcomes.

2. When challenges arise, pause to observe the situation calmly and identify what you can control and what you must accept.

3. Reflect on past experiences where patience and mindfulness helped you grow and apply those lessons to current challenges.

ECHOES FROM THE ZEN GARDEN

Question for Introspection

How can practicing patience in your daily life help you weather challenges and embrace growth?

Story 5:
Breath of the Buddha

In the tranquil seaside town of Kamakura, where ancient temples dotted the landscape and the sea whispered age-old secrets, there resided an old monk named Kaito. Known for his profound serenity and deep understanding of Zen teachings, Kaito had devoted his life to the exploration of mindfulness through the simplest and most universal act: breathing.

Mina, a stressed corporate lawyer from bustling Tokyo, found herself at Kaito's modest temple, driven by a need for respite and a desire to find peace amidst the chaos of her high-pressure career. She was welcomed by the sight of the monk seated in the temple's garden, his eyes closed, his face a portrait of calm.

"Welcome, Mina-san," Kaito greeted, his voice as soothing as the ocean breeze. "I understand you've come to find peace. Let us begin with the very essence of life: our breath."

Intrigued and somewhat skeptical, Mina followed Kaito's gentle command to sit beside him on the smooth stone bench, overlooking the temple's koi pond. The garden around them was a burst of colors, with cherry blossoms gently fluttering to the ground, their brief lives a testament to impermanence.

"Watch the koi," Kaito began, pointing to the fish gliding effortlessly beneath the pond's glassy surface. "They do not think of breathing; it is simply a part of their being. So it must be with us. But first, we must become aware of our breath, something we so often take for granted."

Kaito guided Mina through the process of mindful breathing. "Breathe in deeply, and know that you are breathing in. Breathe out slowly, and know that you are breathing out. Feel the air as it enters and leaves, notice the pause between each breath. This is the foundation of mindfulness."

As Mina followed Kaito's instructions, she began to notice aspects of her breath she had never paid attention to before—the coolness of the air on her nostrils, the rise and fall of her chest, the natural pause at the end of each exhale. Each breath became a world of sensations, and slowly, the cacophony of her thoughts began to quiet.

"Mindfulness of breath brings us back to the present moment, the only moment where life truly exists," Kaito explained, his gaze reflecting the serene depths of the pond. "Like these cherry blossoms, our thoughts are fleeting. They drift past us like petals on the wind. Do not chase them; return to your breath."

Over the following weeks, Mina visited Kaito regularly, each session deepening her practice of mindfulness. They sat together, sometimes in silence, sometimes discussing the subtleties of Zen teachings, but always returning to the breath.

One day, as they sat watching the early signs of autumn ripple through the garden, Kaito spoke of the *Anapanasati Sutta*, the Buddha's discourse on mindfulness of breathing. "The Buddha taught that this practice could lead to profound insights and liberation of the mind. By focusing on our breath, we anchor ourselves in the now, allowing our past and future to dissolve into the rhythm of our breathing."

Mina felt a shift within herself. The constant pressure and stress of her legal career began to lose its grip on her psyche. She found herself more patient, more focused, and significantly less reactive. Her colleagues noticed a change too; there was a new calm in her demeanor, a presence that had not been there before. Inspired by her transformation, Mina decided to incorporate mindfulness into her daily routine. Before important meetings, during lunch breaks, even in the midst of heated negotiations, she would take a moment to focus on her breath, to center herself in the present.

Months passed, and Mina's practice grew deeper, more intuitive. She began to see the breath as a metaphor for life itself—each inhale a new beginning, each exhale a letting go of what no longer served her.

As the season cycled back to spring, and another cherry blossom season graced the temple garden, Mina sat with Kaito, now not just as a teacher and student, but as fellow practitioners of the way of mindfulness. "Kaito-san," Mina said one crisp morning, the air fragrant with blooming flowers, "I came seeking peace from the noise of the world, but I found a peace within, in the silence of the breath."

Kaito smiled, his eyes reflecting the pink blossoms above. "Mina-san, you have discovered the Breath of the Buddha, the silent pulse of the present moment. Carry this with you, and no matter where you are, peace will always be as close as your next breath." Mina left the temple that day with a heart full of gratitude. The teachings of Kaito, the simple yet profound act of mindful breathing, had not only changed her life; they had given her a new way to experience the world, one breath at a time. As she returned to Tokyo, the cherry blossoms swirling around her seemed to whisper a timeless truth—that in the breath, in the present, lies the heart of all peace.

Thought-Provoking Insights

Breathing is the simplest and most universal act of life, yet it holds the profound power to anchor us in the present moment. Mindful breathing connects us to our inner calm, allowing us to release past regrets and future anxieties. Like the fleeting cherry blossoms, thoughts come and go, but by returning to the rhythm of our breath, we find the stillness that exists within us at all times.

Guidance for Application

1. Begin each day with 5 minutes of mindful breathing, observing the sensation of your breath as it flows in and out.

2. In stressful situations, pause and take three deep, intentional breaths to ground yourself in the present.

3. Use your breath as an anchor during moments of distraction, bringing your focus back to the here and now.

ECHOES FROM THE ZEN GARDEN

Question for Introspection

How can focusing on your breath help you navigate moments of stress or overwhelm?

Section 2:
Self-Reflection

Story 1:
The Mirror of the Mind

In the ancient city of Varanasi, a place woven with the fabric of countless pilgrimages and spiritual awakenings, there lived an elderly sage named Deva. Known far and wide for his wisdom and deep introspection, Deva spent his days on the banks of the Ganges, absorbed in the art of self-reflection.

Anita, a young documentary filmmaker from the vibrant city of Mumbai, journeyed to Varanasi to explore the spiritual undercurrents of India for her latest project. She was particularly intrigued by the stories of Deva, whose life's work resonated with the theme of her documentary—understanding one's true self.

Upon reaching Varanasi, Anita found Deva seated serenely amidst the bustling activity of the ghats, his presence a calm oasis. As she approached, Deva opened his eyes, and with a gentle smile, he invited her to sit by his side.

"Welcome, Anita," Deva said, having learned her name through the small talk with locals as she approached. "What seeks you in the labyrinth of the self?"

Anita explained her project and expressed her desire to delve deeper into the concept of self-reflection, hoping to capture its essence on film. Deva nodded thoughtfully and proposed a unique approach to her quest.

"Join me for a day in the life of reflection. Observe your thoughts, emotions, and actions as they unfold. Tonight, we will discuss what you've seen in the mirror of your mind," Deva suggested.

Eager to understand the process, Anita agreed. The day that followed was transformative. Deva guided her through various scenarios—from meditative walks along the river to engaging with the local vendors and pilgrims—each designed to provoke and evoke a spectrum of thoughts and feelings.

Throughout the day, Anita became increasingly aware of her internal reactions. She noticed her initial discomfort with the overt spirituality of the city, her impatience with the slower pace of life, and a surprising sense of peace during a spontaneous conversation with a group of pilgrims sharing their stories.

As the sun began to set, painting the sky with hues of gold and orange, Anita and Deva sat under the shade of an ancient banyan tree to reflect on the day's experiences.

"Let us explore what you've observed, Anita," Deva began, his voice both inquiring and gentle. "What did the mirror of your mind reveal?"

Anita shared her observations, noting how her upbringing in a cosmopolitan city had shaped her perceptions and preconceptions. She spoke of her struggle to connect with her deeper emotions, often masked by the daily grind and her professional persona.

Deva listened intently, then spoke. "Self-reflection is not just about understanding actions but also the roots of these actions. Why do we feel what we feel? Why do we choose one path over another? These questions lead us to a deeper understanding of our true nature."

He continued, "Every thought and emotion has a story. Learn to listen to these stories without judgment. This is how we hold a mirror up to our soul."

Motivated by Deva's insights, Anita spent several more days in Varanasi, each day dedicated to a specific aspect of self-reflection. She documented not only her own journey but also the practices of local ascetics and spiritual seekers, weaving a rich tapestry of introspective narratives.

Her interactions varied widely, from discussing life choices with a young ascetic who had renounced worldly possessions to capturing the silent meditations of older pilgrims seeking moksha, or liberation. Each story added depth to her understanding of self-reflection, painting a vivid picture of how it differed from person to person.

As her time in Varanasi neared its end, Anita realized that her documentary had evolved into something much more profound than she had originally planned. It had become a personal journey into the depths of her own psyche, mirrored by the stories of those she had met.

On her last evening with Deva, Anita thanked him for the invaluable lessons in mindfulness and introspection. "Your guidance has not only changed the course of my documentary but has transformed how I view myself and the world around me."

Deva smiled, his eyes reflecting the flickering lights of the diyas floating on the Ganges. "The mirror of the mind is the most powerful tool we have for self-understanding," he imparted. "Keep it clean, keep it clear, and it will guide you to your true self, beyond the illusions and distractions of the worldly facade."

Anita left Varanasi with a treasure trove of footage and a deeper, more resonant understanding of self-reflection. Her documentary would go on to inspire others to embark on similar journeys of self-discovery, guided by the profound teachings of the sage by the Ganges.

As she boarded the train back to Mumbai, Anita felt a profound sense of peace and purpose. The journey had taught her the importance of looking inward and the transformative power of the mirror of the mind—a lesson she would carry forward in both her personal life and her creative endeavors.

Thought-Provoking Insights

Self-reflection is like gazing into a mirror that reveals not only our outer image but the hidden depths of our thoughts, emotions, and actions. It encourages us to observe our internal world without judgment, allowing us to understand the roots of our feelings and choices. By holding this mirror steady, we can discover who we truly are beyond societal expectations and personal preconceptions.

Guidance for Application

1. Dedicate time each day to quietly reflect on your thoughts and feelings, journaling what you observe without judgment.

2. When faced with a strong emotion, pause and ask yourself, "Why am I feeling this way?" to uncover its deeper roots.

3. Seek moments of stillness, such as during a walk or meditation, to allow your mind to reveal its insights naturally.

Question for Introspection

What patterns in your thoughts or emotions might be telling you something important about your true self?

Story 2:
The Monk's Burden

In the tranquil reaches of Bhutan, nestled among towering peaks and ancient forests, lay the monastery of Thubten Shedrup Ling. This haven, cloaked in serenity and perpetually shrouded by mists that whispered of old secrets, was home to monks who sought enlightenment through deep meditation and disciplined practice. Among these monks was Tenzin, a young novice whose journey of self-reflection was deeply intertwined with a silent burden he carried.

Tenzin was a dedicated monk, his days marked by the rhythmic chanting of prayers and the meticulous performance of his duties. Yet, beneath his calm exterior, he grappled with an internal weight—unresolved emotions and unspoken words that piled up over the years like heavy stones in a sack.

One crisp morning, as golden rays pierced the monastery's thick mists, Lama Sonam, an elder monk revered for his wisdom, approached Tenzin. Observing the young monk's often somber expressions, Lama Sonam decided it was time for a gentle intervention. "Tenzin, join me for a walk in the mountains tomorrow. It is time you learn the art of letting go," he proposed, his voice echoing softly in the chilly air.

As dawn broke the next day, Tenzin and Lama Sonam embarked on their journey, walking paths carpeted with pine needles and flanked by ancient trees that stood as silent witnesses to centuries of seekers. The natural beauty of their surroundings contrasted sharply with the turmoil within Tenzin.

Lama Sonam began to weave a tale as they ascended the narrow mountain trail. "Years ago," he started, his voice steady and clear, "I met an old monk who carried a heavy sack everywhere he went. Each stone in his sack represented a regret, a grudge, or a sorrow from his past. With each day, he added more stones, and soon his burden grew unbearable."

Tenzin listened, his steps slow and thoughtful, absorbing every word.

"The old monk eventually crossed paths with a wise hermit who noticed his struggle. Upon learning about the sack, the hermit asked, 'Why do you carry stones when you can carry lessons instead?' This simple question struck the old monk profoundly," Lama Sonam continued, pausing to let the message resonate with Tenzin.

Reflecting on the story, Tenzin realized he, too, had been collecting stones—stones of guilt for not meeting expectations, stones of unresolved conflicts, stones of self-doubt. The weight of these stones bent his spirit just as surely as a physical burden might.

As they reached a clearing with a panoramic view of the valley below, Lama Sonam invited Tenzin to sit and meditate on the burdens he carried. "Consider each one," he instructed, "not to chastise yourself but to understand and learn from them."

Tenzin closed his eyes, his mind teeming with thoughts. Slowly, guided by Lama Sonam's words, he visualized each stone, acknowledging its presence and the reason it existed. With deep breaths and a growing sense of clarity, he imagined placing each stone on the ground beside him, feeling lighter with each release.

They spent several hours in meditation, the only sounds the rustle of leaves and distant bird calls. When Tenzin finally opened his eyes, the sun was setting, casting a golden glow that seemed to bless his newfound understanding.

"Do you feel lighter, Tenzin?" Lama Sonam asked, a knowing smile playing on his lips.

"I do, Lama," Tenzin replied, a sense of relief washing over him. "I had not realized how much I had been carrying until I set each stone down."

"Remember, my young friend, the journey of self-reflection is continuous. Each day gives us new stones. It is our choice whether to carry them or to learn from them and leave them behind," Lama Sonam advised, his eyes reflecting the wisdom of his years.

Heartened by his mentor's teachings, Tenzin embraced the practice of self-reflection with renewed vigor. He no longer feared the burdens of his emotions and thoughts. Instead, he learned to face them, understand them, and transform them into lessons of growth and enlightenment. Years later, Tenzin, now a respected Lama himself, often shared the story of the old monk and his sack of stones with new novices. He taught them the value of self-reflection, not as a mere exercise in introspection but as a powerful tool for liberation and inner peace. His teachings on the art of letting go became a cornerstone of wisdom at Thubten Shedrup Ling, inspiring countless others to explore the depths of their minds and spirits. Tenzin's journey from a burdened novice to an enlightened mentor stood as a testament to the transformative power of understanding one's self, making him not only a guide but a beacon of hope and strength to all who walked the path of self-reflection in the shadow of the Bhutanese mountains.

Thought-Provoking Insights

We all carry burdens—regrets, grudges, or self-doubt—that weigh down our spirits and hinder our peace. Through self-reflection, we can identify these burdens, understand their origins, and transform them into lessons. Letting go of emotional weights does not mean ignoring them but learning from them, freeing ourselves to walk lighter and live with greater clarity and peace.

Guidance for Application

1. Reflect on emotional burdens you carry and identify their sources, writing them down to gain clarity.

2. Practice visualizing yourself placing these burdens aside, focusing on the lessons they offer rather than their weight.

3. Make self-reflection a daily habit, allowing yourself to regularly release emotional weights and embrace inner freedom.

Question for Introspection

What burdens are you carrying that you could transform into lessons and let go?

Story 3:
The Two Arrows

In the bustling city of Seoul, where modern skyscrapers tower above ancient palaces, there lived a martial arts instructor named Hwan. Known for his skill in Hapkido and his deep philosophical approach to teaching, Hwan was not just a mentor in physical techniques but also in the mental and emotional disciplines that accompanied martial arts.

Among his students was Ji-hoon, a quick-tempered young man who struggled with control, both in and out of the dojang. Despite his undeniable talent and strength, Ji-hoon's inability to manage his emotions was his greatest adversary, often resulting in conflicts and frustration.

Hwan, observing Ji-hoon's struggles, decided it was time for a more profound lesson in self-reflection. One evening, after a particularly intense sparring session, he called Ji-hoon aside.

"Ji-hoon, do you know the story of the two arrows?" Hwan asked, his voice steady and calm.

Ji-hoon, still catching his breath and nursing a bruised ego from the session, shook his head.

Hwan began, "Buddha once spoke of an allegory where a man is struck by an arrow. The pain he experiences is immediate and physical. But then, if he wonders who shot the arrow, why it was shot, and allows anger or fear to overtake him, he is struck by a second arrow. This second arrow is his reaction, causing suffering that is often greater than the physical pain."

Ji-hoon listened, his forehead creasing as he considered the implications.

"You, Ji-hoon, are often hit by this second arrow," Hwan continued. "Your reactions to defeat, to criticism, to your own mistakes, are more debilitating than the events themselves. This is what you must reflect on."

Hwan proposed a challenge. "For the next month, I want you to keep a journal. After each training session, write not only about what happened but also about your reactions. Reflect on them. Understand why you react the way you do and think about how you could react differently."

Reluctantly, Ji-hoon agreed. Over the next few weeks, he filled his journal with observations. He wrote about the frustrations of losing, the shame of mistakes, and the anger over perceived slights from others.

As he wrote, he began to notice patterns. His anger was often a mask for fear—fear of not being good enough, fear of failure. His shame stemmed from a harsh self-judgment that he would never let others impose on him. Each entry in the journal, each act of self-reflection, acted as a mirror showing Ji-hoon more about himself than he had ever realized.

Halfway through the month, Hwan introduced Ji-hoon to meditation, guiding him to use it as a tool to manage his reactions. "Meditation will help you confront the second arrow," Hwan explained. "It will give you the space to choose your reactions instead of being controlled by them."

Ji-hoon found meditation challenging but enlightening. Sitting in silence, focusing on his breath, he learned to observe his thoughts and emotions without immediately reacting. He began to understand the gap between stimulus and response, and in that gap, he found his power to choose.

As the month drew to a close, Ji-hoon's journal entries changed. They became less about anger and frustration and more about understanding and control. His sparring improved, not just in technique but in his sportsmanship and his ability to remain calm and focused under pressure.

On the last day of the challenge, Hwan sat down with Ji-hoon to discuss his progress. They reviewed the journal together, reflecting on the journey Ji-hoon had undertaken.

"You have learned a valuable lesson, Ji-hoon," Hwan said, pride evident in his voice. "The pain of the first arrow is unavoidable. Life will always have its challenges and pains. But the second arrow—your reaction—is within your control. You have learned to avoid it."

Ji-hoon nodded, a sense of accomplishment washing over him. He felt as though he had been fighting with one hand tied behind his back all his life, and now, finally, he was free to use both hands.

With his newfound understanding, Ji-hoon not only became one of the top competitors in Hapkido but also a more thoughtful, controlled person outside the dojang. His journey of self-reflection, prompted by the allegory of the two arrows, taught him that the battles fought within oneself are often the most crucial and that mastering oneself is the greatest victory of all.

Thought-Provoking Insights

Life inevitably brings challenges and pain, represented by the first arrow. However, much of our suffering comes from the second arrow—our reactions to those challenges. By recognizing and reflecting on our emotional responses, we can learn to pause, understand their roots, and choose healthier ways to respond. This practice empowers us to overcome unnecessary suffering and gain mastery over our inner world.

Guidance for Application

1. When faced with frustration or pain, pause and take a few deep breaths before reacting to create space for thoughtful reflection.

2. Keep a journal to document your emotional responses to daily challenges and identify recurring patterns or triggers.

3. Practice mindfulness or meditation to develop greater awareness of the gap between stimulus and response, allowing you to choose reactions that serve your well-being.

EMILY HARPER

Question for Introspection

How do your reactions to challenges create additional difficulties, and how could you respond differently?

Story 4:
The Empty Boat

Along the verdant banks of the Yangtze River, in a small fishing village shrouded in the early morning mist, lived an old fisherman named Chen. With decades of life etched into the lines of his face, Chen was known not only for his unrivaled fishing skills but also for his profound tranquility, a quality that seemed to emanate from him as naturally as the river flowed.

One day, while preparing his net in the quiet of dawn, Chen was approached by Lin, a young man from the city who had come to the village seeking peace from his chaotic urban life. Lin was immediately struck by the old man's serene demeanor and asked if he could join him for the day.

"Of course, young man," Chen agreed with a gentle nod, sensing the turmoil within Lin and recognizing an opportunity for teaching.

As they rowed out into the calm waters, Chen began to share a lesson from his many years on the river. "Let me tell you about the empty boat," he started, his voice as rhythmic as the oars pushing against the water.

"Imagine you are fishing, and another boat crashes into yours. If there is someone in the other boat, you might yell at them to steer clear. You may curse, and anger may flare. But what if the boat is empty?" Chen paused, allowing the image to settle in Lin's mind.

Lin pondered the question, intrigued. "Well, I suppose I would not be angry at an empty boat."

"Exactly," Chen smiled. "The empty boat does not provoke anger because it is just an empty vessel—it has no intentions. Much of life's suffering comes not from others' actions but from our own reactions. If we can see the provocations of others as empty boats, without personal intentions against us, our interactions change."

Throughout the day, as they continued to fish, Chen elaborated on this philosophy, each word a ripple in the still waters of Lin's soul. He explained how every person's actions are influenced by countless factors—like an empty boat driven by the wind, with no purposeful intention to cause disturbance.

As the sun climbed higher and the day grew warm, a real test of Lin's understanding appeared. Another boat, seemingly adrift, came slowly toward them. Lin watched with a tense body and furrowed brow as it bumped gently against their own.

Remembering Chen's earlier words, Lin took a deep breath and looked at the boat. It was indeed empty, likely having slipped its moorings. "The empty boat," Lin murmured, a smile breaking across his face as he realized the directness of the lesson.

"See," Chen said, nodding approvingly, "life is full of empty boats. How you react determines your path through the waters. Anger, frustration, and blame are often as empty as the boat that hits us."

They spent the rest of the day discussing the implications of the empty boat in other aspects of life—relationships, career, and personal growth. Lin learned to view challenges as opportunities to practice reacting without personalization or projection, embracing each as merely another empty boat on the river of life.

As the evening drew near and they made their way back to shore, Lin felt a profound shift within himself. The peace of the river, the rhythm of the oars, and the wisdom of the old fisherman had opened a new way of seeing the world. He was no longer at the mercy of others' actions; instead, he felt empowered to choose his reactions consciously.

Weeks turned into months, and Lin's visit extended. He became a student of the river, guided by Chen's teachings. He practiced mindfulness and reflection daily, using the metaphor of the empty boat to navigate not only the literal waters but also the metaphorical ones of his relationships and inner conflicts.

Eventually, Lin returned to the city, carrying with him the lessons of the river. He approached life with a newfound calmness and clarity, seeing the empty boats in his interactions and choosing his reactions with the same care Chen had chosen his words.

The story of the empty boat became a cornerstone of Lin's philosophy, a guiding principle he shared in his own teachings, as he later became a mentor to others seeking peace in the tumultuous seas of life. Lin's journey by the river, under the guidance of the wise Chen, reminded him and those he taught that the waters of life are navigable, no matter how many boats may drift our way.

Thought-Provoking Insights
Life is full of "empty boats"—situations or people whose actions may feel provoking but often lack intentional malice. Our suffering is not caused by these actions themselves but by the stories we tell ourselves about them. By understanding that many provocations are as impersonal as an empty boat drifting on a river, we can cultivate peace and choose our reactions wisely.

Guidance for Application

1. When faced with a frustrating situation, pause and ask yourself if the provocation is truly personal or simply circumstantial.

2. Practice mindfulness by observing your emotions without judgment, allowing yourself to respond calmly rather than react impulsively.

3. Use the metaphor of the empty boat as a reminder to let go of unnecessary anger or blame, focusing instead on maintaining inner peace.

Question for Introspection

How can you view a recent conflict or provocation as an "empty boat" and change your reaction?

Story 5:
The Gift of Insults

In a bustling town at the edge of Morocco's Sahara Desert, where the sun sets with a fiery passion against the dunes, lived a young baker named Idris. His bakery was a small haven of delight, known throughout the town for its delicious breads and pastries. Idris was well-liked, but he had a temper that flared as quickly as the ovens he tended.

One day, a disgruntled customer, dissatisfied with the crispness of his loaf, hurled insults at Idris as other patrons watched. The words stung, igniting a fire within Idris that was all too ready to burst forth. However, before he could react, an elderly man, known in the town as Uncle Amin, stepped into the bakery.

Uncle Amin was revered for his wisdom and his calm demeanor in the face of adversity. Seeing the tension, he placed a gentle hand on Idris's shoulder and asked if they could talk once his shift was over. Idris, still simmering with anger but respecting the old man, nodded.

As the sun dipped below the horizon, casting long shadows over the sand, Idris and Uncle Amin sat on worn stools outside the bakery. Uncle Amin asked Idris to tell him about the incident.

"I was insulted, Uncle," Idris said, his voice tight with residual anger. "How should I not be angry when my hard work is thrown back in my face?"

Uncle Amin listened intently, then shared a story. "Many years ago, I learned a valuable lesson from my mentor, a wise old woman of the desert. She told me about a philosopher who, when insulted by others, would respond with kindness. He said that if a gift is not accepted, to whom does it belong?"

Idris pondered this, his brow furrowing. "It remains with the giver," he responded slowly.

"Exactly," Uncle Amin said, a smile playing at the corners of his lips. "An insult is much like a gift. If you refuse to accept it, if you do not allow it to become part of you, it remains with the one who offered it."

The simplicity of the metaphor struck Idris with a clarity he had not expected. They discussed how reacting with anger often did nothing but harm oneself, while choosing to not accept the insult could maintain one's peace.

"Let's try an exercise," Uncle Amin suggested. "Think of each insult as a hot coal. If someone offers it to you, and you choose to hold it, who gets burned?"

Idris imagined his open palm holding a glowing coal, the heat searing his skin. "I do," he admitted, the image powerful in its implications.

"For the next week, practice setting down the coals. Do not carry them with you. When someone offers you an insult, imagine placing it down at your feet, unaccepted."

Idris agreed, curious if such a simple change in perspective could alter his reactions.

Over the following days, Idris faced several challenges—customers with complaints, a vendor who shortchanged him, even a stray dog that toppled his trash can. Each time, he pictured the coal. Sometimes he felt the heat before he remembered to set it down, but as the days passed, the coals grew cooler quicker, and his reactions became less heated.

At the end of the week, Idris met again with Uncle Amin, sharing his experiences. "It was not easy, but each time I remembered the coal, I felt a little more in control. It's strange, but I felt less burdened, even relieved."

Uncle Amin nodded, pleased. "You've started to see the power of your own choices, Idris. Each time you refuse to accept an insult, you are choosing peace. You are choosing your own well-being over the fleeting satisfaction of retaliation."

Encouraged by his progress, Idris continued to practice this new approach. The bakery became a brighter place, not just for Idris but for everyone who entered. His staff noticed the change, experiencing less stress and enjoying a more harmonious work environment.

Months turned into years, and Idris's reputation grew—not just for his delicious breads but also for his remarkable temperament. People came not only to buy his pastries but also to experience the peace that had become his bakery's hallmark.

Reflecting on his journey, Idris often shared the lesson of the unaccepted gift with young apprentices, hoping to inspire them as Uncle Amin had inspired him. His story became woven into the fabric of the town, a tale of transformation that reminded everyone that the power of peace lies within, in the choices we make and the insults we do not accept.

Thought-Provoking Insights

An insult, like an unwanted gift, only holds power if we choose to accept it. By refusing to internalize others' negativity, we protect our peace and prevent unnecessary suffering. Reacting with anger burdens us, while letting go fosters resilience and clarity. The power to remain calm lies in recognizing that we control our reactions, not the actions of others.

Guidance for Application

1. Visualize insults or provocations as objects being handed to you. Choose to let them fall rather than hold onto them.

2. When faced with anger or frustration, take a moment to breathe deeply and remind yourself that you control your reaction.

3. Reflect daily on interactions where you successfully let go of negativity, reinforcing the habit of choosing peace.

Question for Introspection

How can you practice "refusing the gift" when faced with criticism or provocation?

Section 3: Positive Thinking

Story 1:
The Sunlit Path

In the heart of the Andes, where the mountains scrape the belly of the sky and the air is crisp with the scent of pine, there lived an elderly woman named Elena. Elena was a weaver of great renown in her village, not only for the vibrant textiles that flowed from her loom but also for the positivity she wove into the very fabric of her community.

Her small cottage was perched on a sunlit path that led to a tranquil meadow, a place where villagers often found respite from their troubles. It was said that a conversation with Elena could turn the darkest clouds into the brightest sunshine.

One chilly morning, a young man named Luis approached Elena's cottage with a heavy heart. Luis was a teacher in the village school, but recent events had left him disheartened. The school's funding had been cut, resources were scarce, and his students' spirits—and scores—were falling.

Elena welcomed Luis into her home with a warm smile and the comforting aroma of coca tea. As they sat by the fireplace, Luis poured out his worries, his words tumbling like the cascades down the nearby mountainside.

"Elena, how do you remain so positive in the face of adversity?" Luis asked, genuinely puzzled by Elena's unwavering cheerfulness.

Elena's eyes twinkled as she placed a comforting hand on Luis's shoulder. "Let me tell you a story, my friend," she began, her voice soft yet filled with a strength that seemed to echo the mountains around them.

"Many years ago, when I was about your age, a disease swept through our village, much like the troubles you face now. It was a dark time, and many fell ill, including my beloved husband. Every night, I feared he would not see the morning. But every morning, I chose to believe he would get better. And you know what? Slowly, he did."

Luis listened intently, his eyes locked on Elena's calm face.

"Every day, I had a choice," Elena continued. "I could dwell on my fears or I could find the strength to hope and to act positively. I wove bright colors into my textiles, even when my heart was gray. And somehow, the act of choosing positivity, of spreading it through my weaving, brought light not only to my family but to the village as well."

Luis pondered this, the simplicity and power of Elena's words stirring something within him.

Elena sipped her tea, then added, "Positivity, Luis, is like the sunlit path outside. It does not remove the mountain; it does not clear the meadow of stones. But it lights up the place where you stand and makes the journey onward less daunting."

Inspired, Luis spent the rest of the day with Elena, learning the basics of weaving. Each thread he added was a decision to infuse his teaching with the same positivity that Elena brought to her craft. They discussed ideas for the school, ways to bring light into his classroom with limited resources, focusing on what could be done rather than what couldn't. As the day turned into evening, and the sun dipped behind the peaks, casting long shadows on the path, Luis felt a renewal of purpose. He thanked Elena for her wisdom and her time, a plan forming in his mind.

Over the next weeks, Luis implemented changes in his classroom. He introduced more creative, low-cost activities that engaged his students in ways the standard curriculum could not. He shared stories of resilience and hope, much like Elena's, and encouraged his students to see problems as challenges to overcome, not barriers to their success. Slowly, the atmosphere in his classroom transformed. Students who had been listless and disengaged began to participate with enthusiasm. Their laughter and excitement filled the room, and their academic performance gradually improved.

Word of Luis's success spread throughout the village, bringing with it a renewed sense of community and a collective effort to support the school. Local artisans, inspired by Luis's example, contributed materials and time. Parents became more involved, and slowly, the school became a center of not just learning, but of hope and positive energy.

Years later, Luis looked back on that morning with Elena as the turning point in his life. He had walked into her cottage burdened by negativity and walked out on a path lit by the sunlight of her wisdom. Elena's legacy of positivity continued to inspire not just him but also his students, long after they had left his classroom.

Luis often told new students about the power of positive thinking, about the sunlit path, and about how, even in the darkest times, choosing to see the light can make all the difference. His story, like Elena's, became woven into the fabric of the community, a lasting testament to the transformative power of a positive perspective.

Thought-Provoking Insights
Positivity doesn't eliminate challenges, but it transforms how we approach them. Like a sunlit path, it illuminates possibilities, providing clarity and hope amidst difficulties. Choosing positivity isn't about denying hardship but about finding the strength to act and inspire others. When we focus on the light, we can uplift not only ourselves but also those around us, creating a ripple of hope and resilience.

Guidance for Application

1. Identify one small, positive action you can take daily to improve your mindset or circumstances.

2. Surround yourself with uplifting stories, people, or activities that inspire hope and creativity.

3. Focus on solutions rather than problems, celebrating small wins along the way to motivate yourself and others.

Question for Introspection

How can you bring a sense of positivity to a current challenge in your life?

Story 2:
The Laughing Buddha

In the heart of Hoi An, a city alive with vibrant colors and the gentle hum of daily commerce, there lived an elderly man known affectionately as the Laughing Buddha. Bao, as he was formally called, was not a Buddha by any stretch of religious implication, but his round belly and ever-present smile drew a charming parallel. He owned a small tea shop on the bustling street of Tran Phu, where the fragrance of jasmine tea mingled with the salty air from the nearby sea.

Bao's tea shop, draped in strings of soft yellow lanterns and adorned with bamboo chairs, was more than a place for refreshment—it was a sanctuary where laughter flowed as freely as the tea he poured. People from all walks of life found solace in Bao's joyful demeanor and the optimistic wisdom he shared.

One sultry evening, as the sun dipped below the horizon, painting the sky in strokes of orange and pink, a young woman named Mai wandered into Bao's shop. With furrowed brow and a restless aura, she seemed out of place amid the usual cheeriness. Mai had recently graduated from university and was grappling with the daunting realities of job hunting and looming adulthood. The pressures had dimmed her spirit, and she carried the weight of the world on her shoulders.

Observing her discomfort, Bao poured a cup of his finest jasmine tea and invited her to sit at a small table near the open window. "What brings such a cloud over your head on such a fine evening?" he inquired, his voice as warm as the tea he offered.

Mai sighed, unloading her burdens of uncertainty about the future and her fear of not living up to expectations. Bao listened intently, nodding in understanding, his smile never fading.

"Ah, I see," Bao responded after a thoughtful pause. "But, dear Mai, let me tell you about the true power of laughter and how it can clear the skies above you."

Bao then shared his philosophy, woven through a story from his own life. "Years ago, before I was the tea master of this little shop, I was much like you—full of worry and doubt. Then, an old monk told me a story about laughter being a prayer that brightens the heart and dispels all shadows. He taught me to laugh, not at others, but at my own predicaments, to find the humor in my missteps and the joy in everyday absurdities."

Motivated to impart this lesson practically, Bao recounted an incident that had transformed his outlook. "One stormy night, much like tonight, I dropped a tray of my most cherished teacups. As they shattered on the tile floor, instead of succumbing to despair, I laughed. I laughed because I realized that those cups were already broken from the moment I first fired them in the kiln—they were impermanent, just like our troubles."

Mai listened, her interest piqued by Bao's unconventional wisdom.

"From that night on, I chose laughter as my companion," Bao continued. "I laughed at my little accidents, at the oddities of life, and soon, I found that my problems didn't disappear, but my perspective of them changed dramatically. I was happier, lighter, and more able to tackle life's challenges."

Inspired by Bao's words, Mai agreed to an experiment. For the next few weeks, she visited the tea shop every evening, engaging in what Bao called "laughter practice." Together, they would recount the day's minor mishaps and twist them into humorous anecdotes. Mai found that as she laughed, her anxiety about job applications and interviews seemed less overwhelming.

As the days turned into weeks, Mai's demeanor brightened significantly. She began to approach her job search with renewed vigor and a positive outlook, applying Bao's teachings. She learned to laugh at the rejections, to see them as necessary steps on her path rather than as setbacks.

Gradually, this shift in perspective brought noticeable changes. Mai's interactions became lighter, and her interviews reflected a confident, cheerful candidate rather than a desperate job seeker.

Ultimately, her positive energy was infectious, and she landed a job at a creative firm that valued her spirited approach.

Years later, Mai, now successful and fulfilled in her career, often looked back at those transformative weeks with Bao. She had not only found a job but had also discovered a lifelong approach to challenges—laughter and positivity.

Bao, the Laughing Buddha of Hoi An, continued to serve his tea and wisdom, reminding all who visited that while life might serve lemons, one could always choose to make lemonade—or better yet, to laugh and make a sweet, refreshing tea.

Thought-Provoking Insights

Laughter is a powerful tool for resilience and perspective. It doesn't eliminate challenges but transforms how we perceive them, lightening the burdens we carry. By embracing humor, especially in the face of setbacks, we can shift our focus from fear and frustration to joy and acceptance. Laughter allows us to find strength and clarity in life's imperfections, turning obstacles into opportunities for growth.

Guidance for Application

1. Reflect on a recent mistake or setback and try to find its humorous or absurd side to diffuse its emotional weight.

2. Practice sharing lighthearted moments with friends or family, focusing on the joy of connection and shared laughter.

3. When overwhelmed, pause and remind yourself that life's imperfections are part of its charm—choose to laugh rather than despair.

Question for Introspection

How can you use humor and laughter to change your perspective on a current challenge?

Story 3:
The Fortunate Misfortune

In the rolling hills of Tuscany, where olive trees and vineyards stretched to meet the horizon, there was a small village called Monteverde. It was a quiet place, where life moved at the unhurried pace of the seasons. Among its residents was a farmer named Marco, known throughout the village for his resilience and good cheer.

Marco lived on a modest piece of land with his wife, Sofia, and their son, Luca. His life was simple, but he found great joy in his work, his family, and the natural beauty surrounding him. However, one autumn, a storm swept through Monteverde, bringing heavy rains and fierce winds that ravaged Marco's farm. The storm destroyed his crops, flooded his fields, and left him staring at a barren expanse where his livelihood once thrived.

The villagers, sympathetic to Marco's plight, came to offer their condolences. "Such misfortune, Marco," they said. "How will you recover from this?"

Marco, standing in the middle of his flooded field, shrugged and said, "Maybe it's misfortune, or maybe it's not. Only time will tell."

His calm demeanor surprised the villagers, but they attributed it to shock. Yet Marco truly believed in waiting to see how events unfolded before labeling them as good or bad.

A few weeks later, while Marco was clearing debris from the storm, he noticed something unusual in the soil. As he dug deeper, he unearthed a vein of clay—a rich, reddish-brown clay that potters from nearby towns prized for their work. Word spread quickly, and soon potters were visiting Marco's farm, eager to buy the clay.

The same villagers who had pitied Marco now came to marvel at his newfound fortune. "How lucky you are, Marco!" they exclaimed. "The storm was a blessing in disguise."

Again, Marco shrugged and said, "Maybe it's good fortune, or maybe it's not. Only time will tell."

With the money he earned from selling the clay, Marco reinvested in his farm, buying seeds, tools, and livestock to replace what he had lost. He even managed to expand his land, planting new crops and building a barn. For a time, life was prosperous, and the farm thrived.

One day, while tending to the fields, Luca, Marco's son, fell from a horse and broke his leg. The injury was severe, and Luca would need months to heal. The villagers, seeing the family's distress, came to offer their sympathy. "What a terrible misfortune, Marco," they said. "Your son will be unable to help you on the farm."

Marco, as always, remained composed. "Maybe it's misfortune, or maybe it's not. Only time will tell," he replied.

The weeks passed, and Luca's leg began to heal. One morning, a group of soldiers arrived in the village, announcing that all able-bodied young men were being conscripted into the army to fight in a distant war. The villagers were filled with dread as their sons were taken away. But because of his injury, Luca was spared from conscription.

The villagers, now struck by the cruel twist of fate, came to Marco and said, "How fortunate you are, Marco. Your son's injury saved him from the war."

Marco nodded, his familiar refrain on his lips. "Maybe it's good fortune, or maybe it's not. Only time will tell."

The war raged on, bringing grief to many families in Monteverde. But Marco's farm flourished, and his family remained together, finding strength in their resilience and gratitude in their blessings.

Years later, as Luca grew into a young man, he would often reflect on his father's calm wisdom. "Papa," he once asked, "how were you able to stay so positive when so many things went wrong?"

Marco smiled and gestured to the olive trees swaying gently in the breeze. "Life is like these trees, Luca. They bend with the wind, but they do not break. What seems like misfortune today may bring blessings tomorrow, and what appears to be good fortune may carry hidden challenges. The key is to embrace it all with an open heart and a steady mind."

Luca carried his father's lesson with him, sharing it with his own children and teaching them to see life not as a series of disconnected events but as a flowing river where every twist and turn contributes to the greater journey.

Marco's story became a legend in Monteverde, a reminder of the power of perspective and the importance of seeing beyond the immediate to find the fortunate misfortunes and hidden blessings in life.

Thought-Provoking Insights
Life is a series of interconnected events, and what seems like misfortune or good fortune in the moment may reveal its true significance only with time. By approaching challenges and blessings with equanimity, we can weather life's uncertainties with grace. True wisdom lies in recognizing that every twist and turn contributes to our journey, shaping us in ways we may not immediately understand.

Guidance for Application

1. When faced with setbacks, remind yourself that their full impact will only become clear with time, and remain open to unexpected outcomes.

2. Reflect on past experiences where initial misfortunes led to growth, opportunity, or unforeseen benefits, and use those lessons to reframe current challenges.

3. Practice mindfulness and gratitude to stay grounded, embracing both joys and difficulties as integral parts of life's journey.

Question for Introspection

How can you embrace life's uncertainties and trust that even challenges may carry hidden blessings?

Story 4:
The Changing Seasons

In a small village nestled at the foot of the Himalayas, where snow-capped peaks touched the heavens and rivers carved their way through valleys, there lived a man named Arjun. Known for his meticulous farming and quiet demeanor, Arjun had a deep connection with the rhythms of nature. Yet, beneath his calm exterior, he struggled with one thing—accepting change.

Arjun's farm was his pride and joy. For years, he had grown the same crops—wheat and barley—reaping steady harvests. He took comfort in the predictability of the seasons and the reliability of his methods. But one fateful year, everything changed. The rains came late, and when they finally arrived, they were torrential, flooding his fields and washing away months of hard work.

The villagers sympathized with Arjun's plight, but many of them had diversified their crops or adopted new techniques. Arjun, however, clung stubbornly to his old ways, convinced that the next season would restore the balance he had always relied on.

That winter, as snow blanketed the village, Arjun visited the home of a wise elder named Kiran. Known for her ability to offer insight through stories, Kiran welcomed Arjun warmly, sensing his frustration and sorrow.

"Tell me, Arjun," Kiran began as they sat by the fire, "what troubles you so deeply that it has brought you here on this cold night?"

Arjun poured out his heart, speaking of the flood, his failed harvest, and his reluctance to change his ways. "I have always trusted the seasons, Kiran," he said, his voice heavy. "But now it feels as though they have betrayed me."

Kiran listened patiently, then began to tell a story. "Many years ago, when I was young, my family planted orchards. We had rows of apple trees that flourished under the sun and rains. One year, a bitter frost came early and killed half the trees. My father was devastated, much like you are now."

Arjun leaned forward, captivated by Kiran's words.

"Rather than despair, my father planted peach trees alongside the surviving apples. He said, 'The seasons are not here to serve us; we are here to adapt to them.' The following year, the apples bore little fruit, but the peaches thrived. And so, our orchard survived by embracing change."

Kiran paused, allowing her words to sink in. "Arjun, the seasons are like life—they are ever-changing. Clinging to what worked yesterday may not serve you today. Sometimes, we must plant new seeds, not knowing what will grow, but trusting the earth to guide us."

Arjun spent the winter reflecting on Kiran's story. As the snow melted and the rivers swelled with spring, he resolved to embrace change. He sought advice from other farmers in the village, learning about crop rotation, flood-resistant seeds, and methods to better manage water flow.

That year, Arjun planted not just wheat and barley but also rice in the lowlands and lentils on the drier slopes. He built channels to redirect floodwaters and mulched his fields to retain moisture during dry spells.

The transformation was not easy. There were days of doubt and hard labor, but Arjun persisted. When the monsoon arrived, bringing both rain and the threat of floods, his farm weathered the storms better than it ever had before. The rice thrived in the waterlogged areas, and the lentils proved hardy during a brief dry spell.

The harvest that year was abundant, not just in crops but in lessons. Arjun had learned to adapt, to see the changing seasons not as adversaries but as opportunities for growth. The villagers noticed the change in him—not just in his farming but in his outlook on life.

One evening, as the village gathered for a festival celebrating the harvest, Kiran approached Arjun, her eyes twinkling with pride. "You have learned the lesson of the seasons, Arjun," she said. "You now understand that life is not about resisting change but about flowing with it, like the rivers that carve their way through stone."

Arjun smiled, the weight of his past fears lifted. "Your story opened my eyes, Kiran. I now see that each season, with its challenges and gifts, is a part of life's greater cycle." From that year forward, Arjun became a source of inspiration for the village. He shared his knowledge of adaptive farming, encouraging others to embrace change and find opportunities in uncertainty. His farm flourished, not because the seasons were kind, but because he had learned to work with them, accepting their unpredictability as a natural part of life. Years later, Arjun would often sit under the shade of a peach tree, planted in honor of Kiran's wisdom. Watching the changing seasons, he would reflect on how the greatest growth often comes from the willingness to let go of the old and embrace the new, trusting that each change, like the turning of the seasons, brings its own kind of harvest.

Thought-Provoking Insights

Change is as inevitable as the shifting seasons, and resisting it often leads to struggle. Like the farmer who adapts to unpredictable weather, we too must learn to adjust our approach to life's challenges. Embracing change opens the door to resilience and growth, allowing us to thrive in the face of uncertainty by seeing every shift as an opportunity rather than a setback.

Guidance for Application

1. Reflect on areas in your life where you are resisting change, and identify one small step you can take to adapt instead.

2. Seek advice or learn from others who have successfully navigated similar challenges, drawing inspiration from their experiences.

3. Remind yourself that each change brings a new set of possibilities, focusing on the opportunities rather than the losses.

/ ECHOES FROM THE ZEN GARDEN

Question for Introspection

How can you adapt to a recent change in your life to find growth and opportunity?

Story 5:
The Full Bowl

In the heart of Kyoto, where ancient traditions danced gracefully with modern life, lived a humble potter named Haruto. His small studio, tucked away at the end of a winding cobblestone street, was filled with clay, tools, and shelves lined with his delicate creations. Each piece, no matter how small or simple, carried a unique story.

Haruto's pottery was sought after for its elegance and charm, yet he lived modestly, content with his craft and the rhythm of his days. What set Haruto apart wasn't just his artistry but his unwavering gratitude for even the smallest joys in life. His neighbors often marveled at his ability to find happiness in moments others would overlook.

One chilly autumn morning, as crimson leaves blanketed the streets, a young woman named Akiko entered Haruto's studio. Her face was etched with worry, and her movements were hurried, as though the weight of the world rested on her slim shoulders. She introduced herself as a journalist and explained that she had come to interview Haruto about his philosophy on life, which had become a local legend. Haruto welcomed her with a warm smile, offering her tea in a simple clay cup he had made years ago. "Let us talk," he said, his voice calm and inviting. "But first, tell me, what troubles you?"

Surprised by his perceptiveness, Akiko hesitated before sharing her struggles. She spoke of her demanding job, the endless chase for success, and the pressure to constantly achieve more. "I feel like I'm running a race with no finish line," she confessed, her voice tinged with exhaustion. "No matter how much I accomplish, it never feels like enough."

Haruto listened intently, then reached for a small, unadorned bowl on a nearby shelf. He placed it on the table between them. "Akiko-san," he began, "what do you see?"

Akiko studied the bowl. "It's a simple bowl," she said. "Beautiful in its simplicity, but it's empty." Haruto nodded. "Ah, but that emptiness is its gift. This bowl, in its emptiness, is ready to receive whatever is placed in it—rice, soup, tea. And when it is full, it serves its purpose with grace."

Akiko looked at the bowl, puzzled by the metaphor.

"You see," Haruto continued, "many of us live as though our bowls are never full. We keep adding, chasing more, yet we fail to appreciate what is already there. True contentment comes not from how much we have but from recognizing the fullness of our bowl at any given moment."

Akiko's brow furrowed as she reflected on his words. "But what if the bowl feels empty? What if life doesn't give enough to fill it?"

Haruto smiled gently and gestured to the shelves around them, filled with his handcrafted pottery. "When I first began as a potter, my shelves were often bare. I struggled to sell my work and doubted my abilities. One day, my mentor told me, 'Look at your bowl, Haruto. Even if it holds only air, it is full, for air sustains life. And if it holds nothing, it is still full of potential.'"

He picked up the bowl again, turning it in his hands. "A bowl is never truly empty, Akiko-san. It holds what you choose to see within it. Even in difficult times, there is something to be grateful for—family, a warm meal, a moment of peace."

Over the course of the morning, Haruto shared more of his reflections. He spoke of finding gratitude in everyday moments, in the soft glow of sunrise, in the laughter of children playing in the street, in the quiet satisfaction of shaping clay on his wheel.

Akiko listened, her heart gradually lightening as she began to see her own life through Haruto's perspective. She realized that she had been so focused on what was missing that she had overlooked the abundance already present. In the weeks that followed, Akiko returned to visit Haruto, not just as a journalist but as a friend and student of his philosophy. She began practicing gratitude daily, starting each morning by writing down three things she was thankful for, no matter how small. Slowly, her outlook shifted. The pressures of her job didn't disappear, but they felt more manageable. She found joy in small victories, in shared meals with friends, and in the beauty of the world around her.

When Akiko's article about Haruto was published, it resonated deeply with readers across Kyoto and beyond. People flocked to his studio, not just to purchase his pottery but to learn from his wisdom. Haruto welcomed them all, sharing his stories and his gratitude, one visitor at a time.

Years later, Akiko often credited her transformation to that simple bowl and the lessons it had taught her. She became an advocate for mindfulness and gratitude, helping others see the fullness of their own lives. And in her home, on a small wooden shelf, she kept one of Haruto's bowls—a daily reminder that even in emptiness, there is always something to be grateful for.

Thought-Provoking Insights

A simple bowl, even when empty, teaches us profound lessons about gratitude and contentment. Life's true richness lies not in how much we have but in recognizing the abundance already present. By appreciating what we hold—whether air, potential, or blessings—we shift our focus from scarcity to fulfillment. Gratitude transforms even the smallest moments into sources of joy and meaning.

Guidance for Application

1. Begin a daily gratitude practice by reflecting on three things you appreciate, however simple or small they may seem.

2. When faced with challenges, remind yourself of the potential within the moment, focusing on what it can teach or offer.

Surround yourself with reminders—like a physical object or note—that encourage you to see fullness and abundance in your life

ECHOES FROM THE ZEN GARDEN

Question for Introspection

What does your "bowl" hold today, and how can you find gratitude in it, no matter how small?

Section 4:
Inner Peace

Story 1:
The Silent Retreat

High in the hills of northern India, nestled among ancient cedar forests, there stood a secluded monastery known as Vana Dhaama, or "The Refuge of the Forest." It was a place where seekers from all over the world came to experience silence—a silence so profound it was said to resonate with the soul's deepest truths.

Meera, a young doctor from Delhi, arrived at Vana Dhaama one crisp autumn morning. The weight of her work in a chaotic hospital, where every second carried the urgency of life and death, had left her spirit battered and her mind restless. Despite her outward composure, Meera felt a gnawing void within, a longing for peace she could not ignore.

The monastery's gatekeeper, an elderly monk named Satyam, greeted Meera with a kind smile but spoke only briefly. "Welcome to the refuge of silence. Here, words are a luxury we set aside to hear what truly matters."

Handing her a simple robe and a set of rules, he led her to a modest room. The walls were bare except for a single window overlooking the forest. "For the next seven days, you will speak no words and hear none," he explained. "You will eat, walk, and breathe in silence. Trust in the stillness—it will guide you."

At first, silence was an unwelcome companion. Used to the constant hum of city life and the relentless chatter of her mind, Meera found the absence of noise almost unbearable. Each hour stretched like an eternity as her thoughts swirled chaotically.

On the second day, Meera joined a group of monks for a silent meal. The act of eating, stripped of conversation, became an entirely new experience. She noticed the texture of the rice, the aroma of the spices, and the satisfying simplicity of chewing. For the first time, she realized how often she had rushed through meals, lost in distractions.

By the third day, Meera began to feel the forest's rhythms. The rustle of leaves, the distant call of a bird, the soft crunch of her footsteps on the forest floor—sounds she had never paid attention to before—now became vivid and alive. Her racing thoughts began to slow, and for the first time in years, she felt truly present.

One evening, as the sun set behind the hills, painting the sky in hues of orange and purple, Meera sat by the monastery's meditation pool. The water mirrored the sky so perfectly that it seemed as if the heavens had descended to meet the earth. As she gazed into the still water, a profound thought surfaced: her mind, too, could reflect such peace if she allowed herself to quieten.

On the fifth day, Meera experienced a moment of clarity so powerful that it brought tears to her eyes. While walking through the forest, she came across an ancient tree, its roots gnarled and exposed, yet its branches reached high, bearing green leaves. The tree, battered by storms and the passage of time, stood unwavering. It was alive, rooted, and thriving despite its scars.

She saw herself in that tree—her struggles, fears, and wounds no longer seemed like burdens to be carried but like roots that had shaped her resilience. In the silence, she realized that peace wasn't the absence of challenges but the acceptance of them.

By the seventh day, the silence that had once felt suffocating had become her sanctuary. Meera felt an inner stillness that she hadn't thought possible. Her breaths came deeper, her heart lighter. The void she had carried for so long now seemed filled with an unshakable sense of calm.

When it was time to leave, Satyam met her at the gate. "How was your silence?" he asked, breaking the quiet with a tone of genuine curiosity.

"It was loud at first," Meera admitted, her voice soft and measured. "But then, it became clear. The silence taught me to listen—not to the noise around me, but to the stillness within."

Satyam smiled, his eyes filled with approval. "That stillness is always with you, Meera. Silence is not something you find; it is something you carry. Let it guide you, even amidst the noise of the world."

As Meera descended the hill and made her way back to the bustling streets of Delhi, she carried with her the profound lessons of Vana Dhaama. Though the city was loud and chaotic, she found moments of quiet in the midst of it all—pausing to breathe deeply, to reflect, and to embrace the silence within. Years later, when Meera spoke of her time at the monastery, she often described it as the most transformative experience of her life. "The silence didn't just change my perspective," she would say. "It gave me the peace I didn't know I was searching for. In the quiet, I found myself." Her story, like the stillness she had discovered, spread far beyond the boundaries of her world, inspiring others to seek their own moments of silence and uncover the inner peace that lay waiting for them.

Thought-Provoking Insights
Silence is more than the absence of sound; it is a doorway to self-awareness. By quieting the external world, we create space to observe our thoughts, understand our emotions, and reconnect with our inner calm. This clarity can help us find peace even in the midst of life's noise.

Guidance for Application

1. Set aside a few minutes daily to sit in silence, focusing only on your breath or the sounds of nature.

2. Create moments of "digital silence" by turning off electronic devices and being present in the moment.

3. Use silence as a tool during difficult situations to reflect before responding.

Question for Introspection

How can embracing silence help you understand your thoughts and emotions better?

Story 2:
The Unmoved Mind

In the windswept plains of Mongolia, where the vast grasslands stretched endlessly beneath a canopy of azure skies, there lived a nomadic herder named Batu. Batu was known for his quiet strength and unshakable calm, traits that had earned him the respect of his tribe. He lived a simple life, tending to his yaks and sheep, guided by the rhythms of nature and the wisdom passed down through generations.

One summer, a young traveler named Aki arrived at Batu's camp. Aki was from the bustling city of Tokyo, and his life had been consumed by the relentless pursuit of success. Exhausted by the pressures of urban life and haunted by his inability to find inner peace, he had journeyed to Mongolia in search of something he couldn't quite name.

Batu welcomed Aki with warmth and curiosity. The traveler, eager to learn, shared his struggles with the nomad over a meal of freshly made dumplings. "I feel like a leaf in the wind," Aki confessed, his voice tinged with frustration. "Every challenge, every failure, tosses me around. I have no control over my own mind."

Batu listened carefully, his eyes reflecting both kindness and deep understanding. "The leaf may be tossed by the wind, but the mountain remains unmoved," he said cryptically. "Stay with me, and I will teach you how to become the mountain."

Intrigued, Aki decided to stay for a while, helping Batu with his daily tasks. The work was hard but grounding—milking yaks, herding sheep, and gathering firewood. Every evening, they would sit by the campfire, and Batu would share stories about the strength of the unmoved mind.

One day, Batu decided to teach Aki a lesson in the form of an exercise. They trekked to a nearby hill, where a large stone rested at the summit. "This stone has been here for centuries," Batu explained. "Storms rage, winds howl, and snow falls, but it remains. Today, you will sit beside this stone, and I want you to watch the wind."

Aki was puzzled but obeyed. He sat beside the stone as the strong Mongolian winds whipped through the grass, tugging at his clothes and hair. At first, he was distracted and restless, his thoughts racing like the clouds above. But as the hours passed, something began to shift. He noticed how the stone stood firm, untouched by the wind's fury. Its presence was calm and steady, a stark contrast to the movement around it.

When Aki returned to the camp that evening, Batu asked him what he had learned. "The stone doesn't fight the wind," Aki said slowly, his words thoughtful. "It simply stays, and the wind moves around it. It doesn't resist."

Batu smiled. "Exactly. Life will always bring storms—unexpected challenges, failures, and sorrows. You cannot control the wind, but you can choose not to be swept away by it. An unmoved mind is like the stone—it observes without reacting."

Over the following weeks, Batu taught Aki techniques to strengthen his mind, starting with simple breathing exercises. "When you breathe, focus on the sensation of air entering and leaving your body," Batu instructed. "This will anchor you to the present moment."

Aki practiced diligently. At first, it was difficult to keep his focus, but gradually, he found himself becoming more aware of his thoughts and emotions. Instead of reacting impulsively, he learned to pause, breathe, and observe.

One afternoon, Batu decided it was time for the next lesson. He led Aki to the riverbank, where the water flowed swiftly over rocks and around bends. "The mind is like this river," Batu explained. "It flows with thoughts and emotions, but you are not the water. You are the observer, watching it pass. The river does not need to stop for you to find peace."

Aki watched the river, absorbing the lesson. He began to understand that inner peace didn't mean eliminating thoughts or emotions but learning to coexist with them without being overwhelmed.

The turning point came one night when a sudden storm swept through the plains. The wind howled, shaking the yurts, and the animals bleated in fear. Aki, initially startled, remembered Batu's teachings. He closed his eyes, focused on his breath, and imagined himself as the stone on the hill—unmoved and steady.

When the storm passed, Aki felt a profound sense of calm. For the first time in years, he wasn't consumed by fear or anxiety. He had found a center within himself, a place untouched by the chaos around him.

As his time with Batu drew to a close, Aki thanked the nomad for his teachings. "You've shown me a strength I didn't know I had," Aki said, his voice filled with gratitude.

Batu smiled, placing a hand on Aki's shoulder. "The strength was always within you. The mountain was there; it simply needed uncovering. Remember, no matter where life takes you, you carry that mountain within."

Aki returned to Tokyo with a transformed outlook. The city was as noisy and fast-paced as ever, but he no longer felt like a leaf in the wind. When challenges arose, he paused, breathed, and anchored himself to the steady presence he had discovered in Mongolia.

Years later, Aki often shared Batu's teachings with others, helping them find their own mountains within. Batu's lesson of the unmoved mind became a guiding principle in his life, a reminder that true peace comes not from controlling the winds but from standing firm and observing as they pass.

> **Thought-Provoking Insights**
>
> Life's storms are unavoidable, but they don't have to disrupt our peace. Like a mountain weathering the elements, we can cultivate inner resilience by choosing to observe rather than react to challenges. Remaining grounded in our values and calm in our responses helps us navigate life with clarity and strength.

Guidance for Application

1. Practice pausing before reacting to stressful situations, allowing yourself time to process emotions.

2. Develop grounding techniques, such as mindful breathing or repeating calming affirmations.

3. Reflect on past challenges and identify how staying calm helped you make better decisions.

EMILY HARPER

Question for Introspection

How can you remain grounded like the mountain when faced with emotional storms?

Story 3:
The Mountain's Stillness

In a remote Himalayan village, surrounded by towering peaks that seemed to pierce the heavens, there lived a shepherd named Arjun. The mountains were his home, his companions, and his teachers. For decades, he had roamed their slopes with his flock, observing their unyielding stillness through sun, snow, and storm.

Arjun was known in his village for his serene demeanor. No matter what troubles befell the community—a poor harvest, an early frost, or disputes among neighbors—Arjun remained as steady as the mountains themselves. When people asked how he maintained his composure, he would simply smile and say, "The mountains have taught me."

One summer, a young traveler named Ravi arrived in the village. Ravi was a scholar from the city, his mind sharp but restless. He had come to the Himalayas in search of peace, hoping to escape the relentless pressures of his academic life.

Hearing of Arjun's wisdom, Ravi sought him out. He found the shepherd perched on a rocky outcrop, watching his sheep graze in the valley below. The two exchanged greetings, and Ravi wasted no time in explaining his plight.

"My mind is like a storm," Ravi admitted, his voice tinged with frustration. "I cannot quiet it. No matter how far I travel, the noise follows me."

Arjun listened patiently, then gestured toward the peaks around them. "You seek peace, but you carry your storm within. Perhaps the mountains can show you what I have learned."

Intrigued, Ravi agreed to stay with Arjun and learn from him. The shepherd set him to work, helping with the daily tasks of tending the flock—guiding the sheep, fetching water, and mending fences. The work was physical but rhythmic, grounding Ravi in a way he hadn't expected.

One morning, Arjun led Ravi to a high plateau, where the mountains loomed large and the world below seemed impossibly distant. "Sit here," Arjun instructed, "and watch the peaks. Observe their stillness."

Ravi did as he was told, though he felt skeptical. The peaks were beautiful, but how could their stillness help him calm his mind? Yet, as the hours passed, Ravi began to notice something. The mountains were not simply still—they were alive in their own quiet way. Clouds drifted around them, snow glistened on their slopes, and shadows shifted with the sun. Despite the movement, their essence remained unshaken.

"The mountains endure," Arjun said, breaking the silence. "They do not fight the wind or the snow. They simply are. Can you learn to be like them?"

Ravi pondered this question as they descended to the village. Over the following days, Arjun continued to teach him through the rhythms of mountain life. When Ravi's thoughts grew restless, Arjun encouraged him to breathe deeply, to feel the earth beneath his feet, and to anchor himself in the present moment.

One evening, as they sat by the fire, Ravi asked, "But what about the storms? Even the mountains face them. How do they remain so unshaken?"

Arjun smiled, tossing a piece of wood onto the flames. "The storms may rage, but the mountain does not resist. It allows the wind to pass, the rain to fall, and the snow to settle. Its strength lies in its acceptance. And when the storm ends, the mountain remains."

The next day, Arjun led Ravi to a hidden cave high in the mountains. Inside, the walls glistened with veins of crystal, reflecting the light of their torches. "This cave," Arjun said, "has weathered countless storms, yet it is untouched. Like the mountain, it holds a stillness within, no matter what happens outside."

Ravi spent hours in the cave, meditating on Arjun's words. For the first time, he felt a glimpse of the stillness the shepherd spoke of—a quiet center within himself that remained, even as his thoughts ebbed and flowed.

As weeks turned into months, Ravi began to change. He no longer sought to silence his thoughts by force but instead let them come and go like passing clouds. He learned to ground himself in the present, finding peace in the simple acts of tending the sheep, watching the sunrise, and feeling the mountain wind on his face.

When it was time for Ravi to leave, he thanked Arjun with deep gratitude. "You've shown me that peace isn't something to chase. It's something to uncover within."

Arjun nodded. "The stillness of the mountain is within you, Ravi. Return to it whenever the storms come, and you will never lose your way."

Ravi returned to the city, but the lessons of the mountains stayed with him. In moments of stress or uncertainty, he would close his eyes and picture the peaks, their unyielding presence grounding him once more. Over time, he shared Arjun's teachings with others, helping them find their own inner stillness amidst the chaos of life.

The story of the shepherd and the mountains became a cherished tale among those who sought peace, a reminder that true calm comes not from avoiding the storms but from finding the unshakable strength within to weather them.

Thought-Provoking Insights

The mountain's stillness teaches us the power of presence and rootedness. Despite external forces, it remains unshaken, embodying balance and tranquility. By finding this stillness within ourselves, we can face life's chaos without being overwhelmed, creating a sense of peace that transcends circumstances.

Guidance for Application

1. Incorporate mindfulness meditation into your routine to train your mind to stay present.

2. Spend time in nature to connect with its stillness and reflect on your own inner balance.

3. Use journaling to identify moments when you felt grounded and explore how to recreate that feeling.

Question for Introspection

What practices can help you cultivate stillness amidst the chaos of daily life?

Story 4:
The Flowing River

In a remote corner of Bhutan, where the emerald hills kissed the sky, there flowed a river named Druk Tashi, the "Dragon's Blessing." The river had long been the lifeblood of the small village of Jangchu, providing water for crops, fish for meals, and a soothing rhythm to the villagers' days. Its waters were clear, its currents steady, and its presence eternal—or so it seemed.

Among the villagers was an elder named Sonam, a man who had spent his entire life by the river's edge. Known for his wisdom and calm demeanor, Sonam often guided others through their struggles with stories and metaphors drawn from the river's movements.

One summer, a young man named Tashi came to Sonam, his face heavy with frustration. Tashi was a carpenter, skilled with his hands but plagued by a restless mind. Despite his talent, he often found himself overwhelmed by his own impatience and anger when things didn't go as planned.

"Sonam-la," Tashi said, addressing the elder with respect, "I don't understand how you remain so calm. Life throws obstacles in my way at every turn. I try to control everything, but the harder I try, the worse things seem to get."

Sonam listened quietly, his expression thoughtful. "Meet me at the riverbank tomorrow morning," he said finally. "Bring nothing but an open mind."

The next day, as the sun began its climb over the hills, Tashi arrived at the riverbank to find Sonam sitting cross-legged on a flat rock. The elder gestured for him to sit beside him. For a while, they simply listened to the gentle rush of the water.

"Do you see this river, Tashi?" Sonam began, his voice soft yet firm. "It flows endlessly, weaving its way around rocks, fallen trees, and narrow bends. It does not stop for obstacles, nor does it fight against them. It simply adapts, finding its way forward."

Tashi frowned, unsure of what this had to do with his struggles. "But it's just a river," he said. "It has no choice but to flow."

"Ah," Sonam replied with a smile, "but so do you. Life flows, Tashi, whether we want it to or not. The choice is in how we navigate it. Many people waste their energy resisting what cannot be changed, trying to control every twist and turn. The river teaches us that peace comes from learning to move with the current, not against it."

To illustrate his point, Sonam picked up a stick and threw it into the river. The current carried it effortlessly, weaving around obstacles and following the path of least resistance. "See how the stick flows?" Sonam said. "It does not fight the water, yet it moves steadily forward."

For the next week, Sonam invited Tashi to join him at the river every morning. Each day, they observed a different aspect of its flow—the way it swirled in pools, the speed of its current in narrow channels, and the stillness in deeper sections. With each lesson, Sonam encouraged Tashi to reflect on his own life.

One morning, after a night of heavy rain, Tashi saw that the river had swollen, its once-gentle current now fierce and wild. "Even the river struggles," he remarked, watching debris rush by in the torrent.

"Not a struggle," Sonam corrected. "This is its nature. It adapts to the rain, expanding to accommodate the storm. And when the rain stops, it will shrink again, calm and steady as before. The river does not resist the storm; it accepts it."

That day, something shifted in Tashi. He began to see his own challenges in a new light—not as barriers to overcome but as parts of life's flow to navigate. He realized that his anger and impatience stemmed from his desire to control everything, a futile effort that only added to his stress.

Over time, Tashi practiced applying the river's lessons to his craft. When a project didn't go as planned, he paused, took a deep breath, and considered how to adapt rather than forcing a solution. He discovered that when he let go of his need for control, his creativity flourished.

One evening, Tashi visited Sonam to share his progress. "The river has taught me more than I ever thought possible," he said, gratitude shining in his eyes. "I no longer feel trapped by my struggles. Instead, I feel like I'm flowing with life, just as the river does."

Sonam nodded, his face lighting up with pride. "You have learned well, Tashi. Remember, the river is always moving, and so is life. Trust the flow, and you will find peace, even in the roughest waters."

As the years passed, Tashi became known in the village not only for his skill as a carpenter but also for his calm and grounded presence. People often came to him for advice, and he would share the lessons he had learned from the river.

The story of Sonam and the flowing river became a cherished tale in Jangchu, passed down through generations as a reminder that life's greatest peace is found not in controlling the current but in learning to flow with it.

Thought-Provoking Insights
The river's flow reminds us that peace comes from adaptability. Life's challenges, like obstacles in the river's path, can be navigated with grace if we learn to move with them rather than resist. By embracing change and trusting the journey, we can find resilience and freedom in life's natural currents.

Guidance for Application

1. Identify a current challenge and brainstorm ways to adapt instead of resisting.

2. Practice visualizing yourself as water, flowing around obstacles with ease and flexibility.

3. When facing difficulties, remind yourself that every challenge is a part of life's natural rhythm.

Question for Introspection

Where in your life can you embrace flow instead of resisting change?

Story 5:
The Lotus in the Mud

In a quiet village in Cambodia, surrounded by emerald rice paddies and tranquil lotus ponds, there lived a woman named Dara. Her name, meaning "star," was a poetic contrast to the life of hardship she had endured. Dara was a widow and mother of two young children, struggling to make ends meet by weaving baskets and selling them in the local market. Life was a constant battle, and Dara often felt overwhelmed by the challenges she faced.

One humid morning, after a particularly difficult night when heavy rains had destroyed several of her freshly woven baskets, Dara walked to the lotus pond near her home. This pond, teeming with the pink blossoms of lotus flowers, had always been her place of solace. As she sat by the water's edge, her mind raced with worry and self-doubt. How would she recover from yet another setback? How could she provide for her children in a world that seemed determined to weigh her down?

Lost in thought, Dara didn't notice an elderly monk approach until he spoke. "The lotus blooms beautifully despite the mud it grows in," he said, his voice calm and steady. Startled, Dara turned to see the monk, his orange robes vibrant against the greenery. He gestured toward the pond. "Do you see those flowers? Their roots are buried in the mud, yet they rise above it, untainted, to bloom in the sunlight."

Dara nodded, her curiosity piqued. "But how?" she asked, her voice tinged with frustration. "How does something so pure and beautiful emerge from such filth?"

The monk smiled. "The lotus does not resist the mud; it uses it. The mud is its foundation, its source of strength. Without it, the lotus could not grow."

Intrigued, Dara listened as the monk continued. "Life's challenges are like the mud. They may seem dirty and unpleasant, but they are the soil in which we grow. Inner peace does not come from escaping life's difficulties but from rising above them, just as the lotus rises above the mud."

The monk's words lingered in Dara's mind long after he left. She began to see her struggles in a new light. Each setback, each moment of hardship, was not a punishment but an opportunity to grow stronger, to rise above the difficulties and bloom like the lotus.

Over the following weeks, Dara returned to the pond daily, sitting quietly and observing the flowers. She noticed how the blossoms opened slowly in the morning sunlight, how their petals remained untouched by the water below. Inspired by their resilience, she began to apply the monk's teachings to her own life.

Instead of dwelling on her losses, Dara focused on what she could do with what she had. She experimented with weaving techniques, creating baskets that were sturdier and more intricate. She taught her children to help her, not as a burden but as a way to share in the family's efforts. Together, they turned their small home into a bustling workshop.

Dara also began practicing mindfulness, a skill she had learned from watching the lotus. She started each day with a quiet moment by the pond, reflecting on her blessings and setting her intentions. When challenges arose, she reminded herself that the mud was part of her growth, not an obstacle to it.

One evening, as the sun dipped below the horizon, painting the sky in hues of gold and crimson, Dara noticed something extraordinary. A lotus flower near the edge of the pond had begun to bloom. Its petals, delicate yet strong, opened fully for the first time. In that moment, Dara felt a deep sense of connection to the flower. She, too, was blooming, rising above her struggles to find beauty and strength in the midst of life's challenges.

Word of Dara's resilience spread through the village, and her baskets became highly sought after, not just for their craftsmanship but for the story they carried. People came to her not only to buy her wares but also to seek her wisdom. She would often share the lesson of the lotus, reminding them that the mud of life's struggles could nourish growth and beauty.

Years later, Dara's children, now grown, carried their mother's teachings with them. They often returned to the pond, where they would sit and watch the lotus flowers bloom, each one a reminder of their mother's strength and the power of inner peace.

The story of Dara and the lotus became a cherished tale in the village, a testament to the idea that even in the darkest and dirtiest of times, one can rise above and bloom with grace and beauty. It was a reminder that peace is not the absence of struggle but the ability to grow through it, untainted and radiant like the lotus in the mud.

Thought-Provoking Insights

The lotus flower blooms with purity and beauty despite growing in muddy waters. Similarly, our greatest growth often stems from life's challenges. By seeing struggles as opportunities for transformation, we can rise above difficulties and cultivate resilience, emerging stronger and more radiant.

Guidance for Application

1. Reflect on a recent hardship and write down the lessons you've learned from it.

2. Practice gratitude for the challenges that have shaped your resilience and character.

3. Use affirmations to remind yourself that growth often arises from adversity

Question for Introspection

What struggles in your life have helped you grow into a better version of yourself?

Conclusion

As we reach the end of *Zen Whispers: Stories of Mindfulness and Serenity*, we reflect on the journey through stories that spoke to the heart of what it means to live fully, with clarity, resilience, and peace. Each tale offered a unique glimpse into the transformative power of mindfulness, self-reflection, positive thinking, and inner peace. Through the experiences of diverse characters, we've learned how simple yet profound practices can guide us through life's challenges.

These stories showed that mindfulness is not about escaping the world but embracing it as it is. Kenji's journey to the brook and Emiko's discovery of the present moment through her art revealed the beauty of being fully present. Mindfulness is about anchoring ourselves in the now, finding joy and calm in even the smallest of acts.

Through self-reflection, we explored the power of looking inward. Tenzin's realization that he could let go of his burdens and Ji-hoon's ability to control his reactions taught us that understanding our inner world is the first step to transforming it. Reflection allows us to see our thoughts and emotions not as fixed truths but as passing waves, each offering a lesson.

The stories of Marco and Akiko demonstrated the power of positive thinking. Marco's resilience through life's ups and downs and Akiko's newfound gratitude showed how optimism can shift our perspective, revealing opportunities where we once saw obstacles. Positivity doesn't erase difficulties, but it gives us the strength to face them with hope and determination.

Inner peace, as seen in Arjun's journey with the changing seasons and Haruto's lesson of the empty bowl, reminded us that calm is not found in controlling the external world but in accepting its unpredictability. Peace is cultivated from within, like a river flowing gently over stones or a bowl filled with gratitude for the air it holds.

Each story was followed by reflections to deepen your understanding, with thought-provoking insights, questions for introspection, and practical guidance. These sections encouraged you to not just read but to actively engage with the lessons, making this book a tool for growth as much as a source of inspiration.

This book is more than a collection of stories; it is an invitation to embrace a way of living that values simplicity, presence, and growth. The lessons are universal, reminding us that no matter our background or circumstances, we all have the ability to transform our outlook and approach life with greater balance.

As you close this book, consider the themes and lessons that resonated most with you. Was it the mindfulness of Emiko's art? The resilience of Marco's spirit? The gratitude of Haruto's simple bowl? Each character faced challenges that mirrored our own struggles, and their stories are a reminder that we, too, can navigate life's uncertainties with grace and strength.

Life will always bring challenges—unexpected storms, shifting seasons, and moments of doubt. But just as Marco learned to adapt his farm and Ji-hoon discovered the power to control his reactions, we can learn to meet these challenges with awareness and resilience. Each obstacle is an opportunity for growth, each struggle a chance to deepen our understanding of ourselves and the world.

Remember, Zen is not about achieving perfection but about cultivating presence and balance. Small actions—a mindful breath, a moment of reflection, a choice to view challenges as opportunities—can ripple outward, transforming not just our lives but the lives of those around us. These principles are not bound by time or place; they are tools for everyday living, accessible to anyone willing to practice them.

Thank you for taking this journey through *Zen Whispers*. Whether you carry the lessons of mindfulness into your daily routine, reflect on your thoughts with curiosity, or find gratitude in life's smallest blessings, know that the wisdom of these stories is always available to guide you. Life is unpredictable, but with awareness, you can meet it with a steady heart and an open mind.

As you move forward, may you find inspiration in these stories to pause, reflect, and grow. Let the whispers of Zen guide you to see the beauty in the present, the wisdom in challenges, and the peace within yourself. The path ahead may be uncertain, but your practice of mindfulness, gratitude, and inner calm will light the way. The world is waiting for the serenity and strength you bring—one mindful step at a time.

Printed in Dunstable, United Kingdom